D1269365

BY LARRY MACK

THE NEW YORK
GIANTS
STORY

BELLWETHER MEDIA · MINNEAPOLIS, MN

Are you ready to take it to the
extreme? Torque books thrust you
into the action-packed world of
sports, vehicles, mystery, and
adventure. These books may include
dirt, smoke, fire, and chilling tales.
WARNING: read at your own risk.

This edition first published in 2017 by Bellwether Media, Inc.

No part of this publication may be reproduced in whole or in part without
written permission of the publisher. For information regarding permission,
write to Bellwether Media, Inc., Attention: Permissions Department,
5357 Penn Avenue South, Minneapolis, MN 55419.

Library of Congress Cataloging-in-Publication Data

Names: Mack, Larry, author.
Title: The New York Giants Story / by Larry Mack.
Description: Minneapolis, MN : Bellwether Media, Inc., 2017. | Series:
   Torque: NFL Teams | Includes bibliographical references and index.
Identifiers: LCCN 2015036713 | ISBN 9781626173750 (hardcover : alk. paper)
Subjects: LCSH: New York Giants (Football team)–History–Juvenile literature.
Classification: LCC GV956.N4 M33 2017 | DDC 796.332/64097471–dc23
LC record available at http://lccn.loc.gov/2015036713

Printed in the United States of America, North Mankato, MN.

TABLE OF CONTENTS

Super Bowl 46 has been a back-and-forth game. The New York Giants took an early lead over the New England Patriots. But now they trail by 8 points in the third quarter.

Eli
Manning

COME FROM BEHIND
The Giants have trailed at halftime in all four of the Super Bowls they have won!

Tom
Coughlin

Giants coach Tom Coughlin
checks the scoreboard. His team
and star **quarterback** Eli
Manning are running out of time.

Ahmad
Bradshaw

The Giants' **offense** marches up the field for two field goals. Now at the end of the third quarter, the team is behind by only 2 points.

Then, the Giants get the ball again. Manning hands it to Ahmad Bradshaw. The **running back** dashes for an easy touchdown. The Giants lead 21 to 17! New England cannot come back. The Giants win their fourth Super Bowl!

SCORING TERMS

END ZONE
the area at each end of a football field; a team scores by entering the opponent's end zone with the football.

EXTRA POINT
a score that occurs when a kicker kicks the ball between the opponent's goal posts after a touchdown is scored; 1 point.

FIELD GOAL
a score that occurs when a kicker kicks the ball between the opponent's goal posts; 3 points.

SAFETY
a score that occurs when a player on offense is tackled behind his own goal line; 2 points for defense.

TOUCHDOWN
a score that occurs when a team crosses into its opponent's end zone with the football; 6 points.

TWO-POINT CONVERSION
a score that occurs when a team crosses into its opponent's end zone with the football after scoring a touchdown; 2 points.

THE NEW YORK FOOTBALL GIANTS

The New York Giants are one of the oldest National Football League (NFL) teams. They joined the NFL in 1925. They were named after the New York Giants baseball team of the time.

1925 season

The Giants are also among the most successful NFL teams. They have been NFL champions eight times!

Since 1976, the Giants have played home games in East Rutherford, New Jersey. The Giants share MetLife Stadium with the New York Jets.

Each week, workers prepare the stadium for the team that is playing. They change banners, lighting, and even the end zone **turf**.

FAMILY TIES

Tim Mara was the Giants' first team owner. Today, Mara's grandson, John, is part owner of the Giants.

EAST RUTHERFORD, NEW JERSEY

METLIFE STADIUM

The Giants are in the National Football **Conference** (NFC). Their **division** is the NFC East. It includes the Philadelphia Eagles, Dallas Cowboys, and Washington Redskins.

The Giants' biggest **rivals** are the Eagles and Cowboys. The Giants also have a hometown rivalry with the Jets.

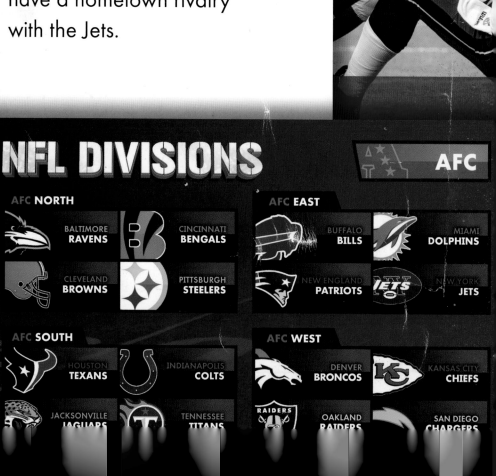

NFL DIVISIONS

AFC

AFC NORTH

BALTIMORE **RAVENS**

CINCINNATI **BENGALS**

CLEVELAND **BROWNS**

PITTSBURGH **STEELERS**

AFC EAST

BUFFALO **BILLS**

MIAMI **DOLPHINS**

NEW ENGLAND **PATRIOTS**

NEW YORK **JETS**

AFC SOUTH

HOUSTON **TEXANS**

INDIANAPOLIS **COLTS**

JACKSONVILLE **JAGUARS**

TENNESSEE **TITANS**

AFC WEST

DENVER **BRONCOS**

KANSAS CITY **CHIEFS**

OAKLAND **RAIDERS**

SAN DIEGO **CHARGERS**

 NFC

NFC NORTH

 CHICAGO
BEARS

 DETROIT
LIONS

 GREEN BAY
PACKERS

 MINNESOTA
VIKINGS

NFC EAST

 DALLAS
COWBOYS

 NEW YORK
GIANTS

 PHILADELPHIA
EAGLES

 WASHINGTON
REDSKINS

NFC SOUTH

ATLANTA
FALCONS

 CAROLINA
PANTHERS

 NEW ORLEANS
SAINTS

TAMPA BAY
BUCCANEERS

NFC WEST

 ARIZONA
CARDINALS

 LOS ANGELES
RAMS

 SAN FRANCISCO
49ERS

 SEATTLE
SEAHAWKS

The Giants' first NFL game was in October 1925. They lost, but quickly got up to speed.

1925 season

THE SNEAKER GAME
Sneakers helped the Giants win the icy 1934 NFL Championship game. The shoes gave them better grip on the slippery field.

In 1927, the Giants had the NFL's best record. Back then, there was no championship game. The Giants were named NFL champions!

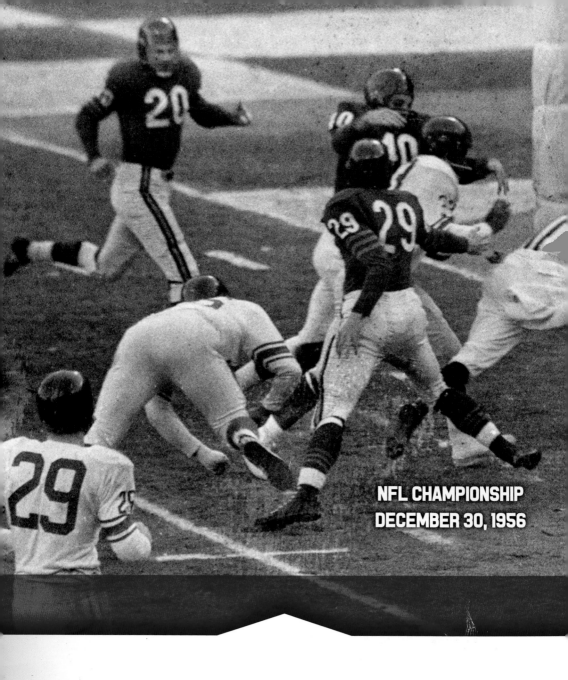

NFL CHAMPIONSHIP
DECEMBER 30, 1956

The Giants won three more championships in 1934, 1938, and 1956. After a 1963 championship loss, they struggled. But in the 1980s, they started making the **playoffs**!

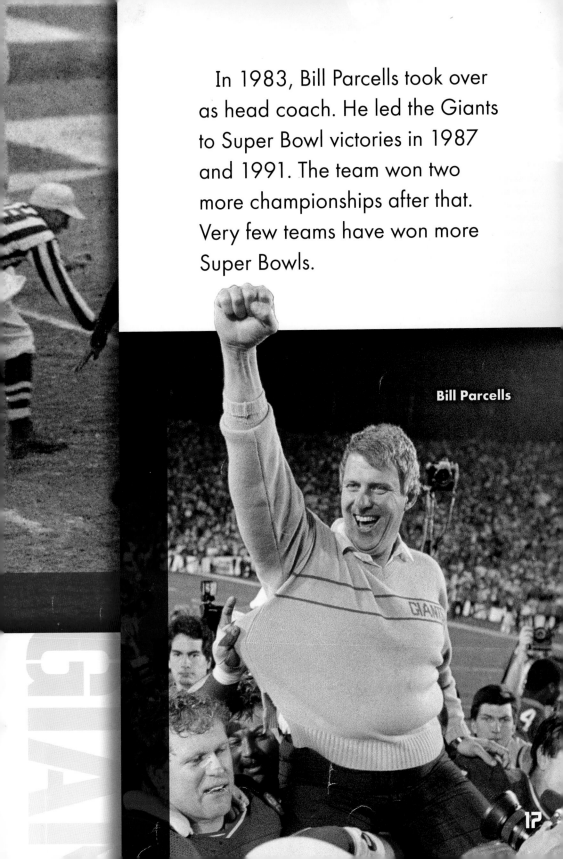

In 1983, Bill Parcells took over as head coach. He led the Giants to Super Bowl victories in 1987 and 1991. The team won two more championships after that. Very few teams have won more Super Bowls.

Bill Parcells

TIMELINE

1925

Played first
NFL game

1927

Claimed the NFL
Championship

1938

Won the NFL Championship,
beating the Green Bay Packers

23 FINAL SCORE **17**

1934

Won the NFL Championship,
beating the Chicago Bears

30 FINAL SCORE **13**

1956

Won the NFL Championship,
beating the Chicago Bears

47 FINAL SCORE **7**

1983

Hired Bill Parcells as head coach

2004

Traded for quarterback Eli Manning at the NFL draft

1987

Won Super Bowl 21, beating the Denver Broncos

39   FINAL SCORE   **20**

2008

Won Super Bowl 42, beating the New England Patriots

17   FINAL SCORE   **14**

1991

Won Super Bowl 25, beating the Buffalo Bills

20   FINAL SCORE   **19**

2012

Won Super Bowl 46, beating the New England Patriots

21   FINAL SCORE   **17**

The Giants have been built on star players. Frank Gifford was a great running back. He reached the **Pro Bowl** eight times. In 1963, quarterback Y. A. Tittle threw a team record 36 touchdown passes.

Frank Gifford

GREATEST CATCH EVER?

Odell Beckham Jr. is a young Giants star. In 2014, he made a famous touchdown catch using only three fingers!

MICHAEL STRAHAN
DEFENSIVE END
1993-2007

AMANI TOOMER
WIDE RECEIVER
1996-2008

ELI MANNING
QUARTERBACK
2004-PRESENT

Football fans all over New England used to cheer for the Giants. Many stayed loyal even after the New England Patriots formed.

Before the Giants, football fans often got more excited about the offense than the **defense**. In the 1950s, Giants fans began cheering for their defense, too. Many say that Giants fans invented the "De-fense!" chant.

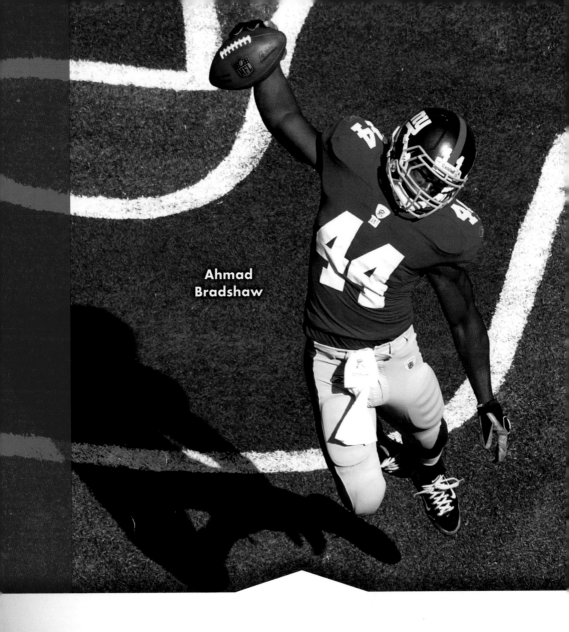

Ahmad
Bradshaw

Giants players started famous traditions, too. In 1965, Homer Jones was the first player to **spike** the ball after a touchdown. The 1985 Giants began dumping Gatorade on their coach after wins. They made the celebration famous.

The Giants give their fans
many reasons to watch the team.
The team cannot win every
Super Bowl. But their fans might
witness a new sports tradition!

MORE ABOUT THE
GIANTS

Team name:
New York Giants

Team name explained:
Named after one of the
city's pro baseball teams
at the time

Nicknames: Big Blue,
New York Football Giants,
G-Men

Joined NFL: 1925

Conference: NFC

Division: East

Main rivals: Dallas Cowboys,
Philadelphia Eagles

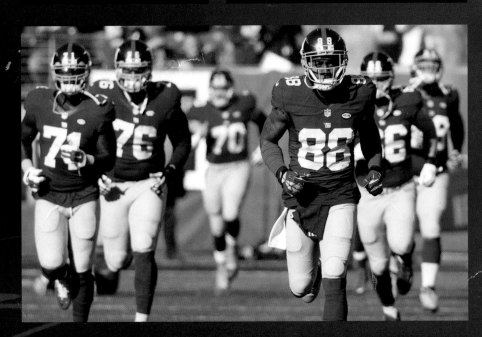

Hometown:
New York, New York

**Training camp location: Quest Diagnostics
Training Center, East Rutherford, New Jersey**

Home stadium name:
MetLife Stadium

Stadium opened: **2010**

Seats in stadium: **82,500**

Logo:
White or blue "ny"

Colors:
Blue, red, white

GLOSSARY

conference—a large grouping of sports teams that often play one another

defense—the group of players who try to stop the opposing team from scoring

defensive end—a player on defense whose job is to tackle the player with the ball

division—a small grouping of sports teams that often play one another; usually there are several divisions of teams in a conference.

linebacker—a player on defense whose main job is to make tackles and stop passes; a linebacker stands just behind the defensive linemen.

offense—the group of players who try to move down the field and score

playoffs—the games played after the regular NFL season is over; playoff games determine which teams play in the Super Bowl.

Pro Bowl—an all-star game played after the regular season in which the best players in the NFL face one another

quarterback—a player on offense whose main job is to throw and hand off the ball

rivals—teams that are long-standing opponents

running back—a player on offense whose main job is to run with the ball

spike—to throw the ball to the ground with force

Super Bowl—the championship game for the NFL

turf—the grasslike surface of a football field

wide receiver—a player on offense whose main job is to catch passes

TO LEARN MORE

AT THE LIBRARY

Whiting, Jim. *The Story of the New York Giants.* Mankato, Minn.: Creative Education, 2014.

Wyner, Zach. *New York Giants.* New York, N.Y.: AV2 by Weigl, 2014.

Zappa, Marcia. *New York Giants.* Edina, Minn.: ABDO Pub. Company, 2015.

ON THE WEB

Learning more about the New York Giants is as easy as 1, 2, 3.

1. Go to www.factsurfer.com.

INDEX